Horseshoes and Trolley Poles

Fintona and Howth trams in the 1950s

Anthony Burges

Colourpoint Books

Horseshoes and Trolley Poles

Dedicated to an old friend Desiree Steadman (neé Buchanan) of Ottawa and formerly of Fivemiletown, Co Tyrone, with family connections to Liskey House, Fintona, Co Tyrone.

First Edition
First Impression

© Anthony Burges and Colourpoint Books 2008

Designed by Colourpoint Books
Printed by GPS Colour Graphics Ltd

ISBN 978 1 906578 24 4

Colourpoint Books
Colourpoint House
Jubilee Business Park
21 Jubilee Road
Newtownards
County Down
Northern Ireland
BT23 4YH
Tel: 028 9182 6339
Fax: 028 9182 1900
E-mail: info@colourpoint.co.uk
Web-site: www.colourpoint.co.uk

After an initial period as a 'mourner' in the fifties at branch line funerals in the UK and Ireland, Tony pursued studies at Southampton University followed by graduate school at Northwestern University, Chicago. His subsequent career in the Canadian government as Transport Policy Advisor in the Department of Finance, Director General, Grain Transportation & Handling, and subsequently Deputy Executive Director, Australian Railway Research & Development Organization earned him the sobriquet of 'Mr Branchline' among his colleagues. Retiring recently from a Washington DC based firm of transportation consultants he is now devoting his time to writing railway books in Ottawa. He is also the author of *Railways in Ulster's Lakeland* and other Irish titles published by Colourpoint Books, as listed on the inside rear cover.

Unless otherwise credited all photographs are by the author.

Front cover:

The Fintona tram en route to Fintona in 1953. (*GR Siviour*)
Hill of Howth tram No 7 at The Summit in 1957. (*Author*)

Rear cover:

Hill of Howth tram No 7 at Baily View loop in 1958. (*GR Siviour*)

Introduction and Fintona

Until 1957 the Great Northern Railway (Ireland) presented the railway enthusiast with a cornucopia of riches in the form of a choice of traction ranging from a rare survival of a horse drawn passenger service, through an array of well maintained steam locomotives both ancient to modern, a vintage electric tramway combining scenic delights with a more mundane commuter role and a definitive display of diesel traction ranging from primitive rail-bus conversions, through ingenious Dundalk built articulated units, to modern multiple units. This book pays special homage to the valiant efforts of the GNRI in maintaining two of the most delightful components of the Irish railway scene in an era when their special qualities were yet to be fully appreciated. It is appropriate that relics of these two most distinctive byways of the Great Northern Railway (Ireland) should be sharing a common roof at the Ulster Folk and Transport Museum at Cultra.

Fintona: A One Horse Town

Small, unassuming and 'slightly off the beaten track' are terms that most aptly describe the quiet community of Fintona, Co Tyrone. In the mid nineteenth century, when the railway arrived, the population was approximately 1,750. More recently, in 2007, the estimated population was 1,384. Nestled in undulating pastoral countryside and drained by streams flowing into the Owenreagh River, which joins the River Strule at Omagh, Fintona is bounded by a range of hills to the south separating it from the Clogher valley with its erstwhile narrow gauge memories.

In the fifties, Fintona was a microcosm of the small Ulster farming community. Its weekly market was declining as a result of competition from nearby Omagh but the town's pivotal location at the hub of a network of secondary roads linking it to Dromore, Enniskillen, Clogher, Omagh and Sixmilecross echoed its former regional significance. The preoccupations of its citizens were related in various ways to the health of the dairying and store cattle sectors and the outlook for the hay, oat and potato crops. The historical importance of the town as a stronghold of the O'Neills was but a distant memory and the proximity of the county town of Omagh, some eight miles distant by road, was a growing force in the life of the community. As in most Ulster agricultural districts, the local farms had been increasingly mechanized and car ownership had risen in recent years. Rural bus services and road haulage were concurrently slowly capturing the traditional business of the railways, a process that was actively encouraged by the policies of the Northern Ireland government. Today the remaining public transport is provided by Translink and is limited to five or six bus journeys on weekdays to nearby Omagh.

The title of this review is not intended as a pejorative characterization of the town, as found in the traditional cowboy films of the time. Horses have always enjoyed a special status and respect in the hearts of the Irish people and it was a single solitary horse that put Fintona firmly on the map and elevated the town from relative obscurity to fame as a mecca for railway enthusiasts from far and wide. For, in addition to the delights of racing, show jumping, hunting and its age-old role as the precursor of the farm tractor, the horse in Fintona represented power for a public transport service; the survival of a tradition dating back to Charles Bianconi, the Italian pioneer of stage coach travel in nineteenth century Ireland. Although there were some isolated remnants of horse traction on the Irish railways which could still be found in the mid twentieth century on short industrial lines such as those at Upperlands, Co Derry and

Shannonvale Co Cork, the distinguishing features of the Fintona branch were that it carried both passengers and freight and was operated by a major railway (the Great Northern). Another notable aspect of the line was its extraordinary longevity with horse traction continuing for more than one hundred years. Perhaps this could be attributed to its limited length of only three quarters of a mile and its restricted role in providing a feeder service connecting to a meandering cross country route. Maybe it was as much a matter of 'out of sight, out of mind' as far as the GNRI management was concerned.

Fintona was connected to the developing Irish railway network on 15 June 1853 when the impecunious Londonderry and Enniskillen Railway established a temporary terminus. The subsequent gradual extension of the line to Enniskillen resulted in Fintona becoming the terminus of a short branch line on 16 January 1854, from a station at Fintona Junction. Recognizing the doubtful economics of steam power on such a short line, authorization was obtained from the Board of Trade to employ horse traction – a state of affairs that continued for nearly 104 years and survived subsequent changes in ownership. As a general rule, only goods traffic in excess of a single wagon was steam hauled. Throughout its existence, two double deck trams were allocated to the line. The first car lasted from 1854 to 1883 and its successor, which was so beloved by townsfolk and visitors, was used until closure on 1 October 1957. With continuous operation for 104 years, the only interruption in service that occurred was from 17 January to 2 April 1953 as a result of damage to the tram (or 'van' as it was locally known) sustained when the horse took fright and bolted. This suspension of service provoked a public outcry when the Great Northern unsuccessfully sought to make it permanent. The decision was quickly reversed and the tram was repaired and returned to service.

The tram is preserved to this day at the Ulster Folk and Transport Museum at Cultra Co Down. There was nothing quite like the horse drawn Fintona tram to be seen elsewhere in Ireland. Platforms at each end gave access to a partitioned saloon which was protected by sliding doors and provided first and second class accommodation, while historically, it was deemed appropriate to confine 'the lower social orders' to the open upper deck. The abolition of second class by the GNRI in 1951 brought the third class passengers in from the cold, as the tram became effectively 'classless', leaving the open air delights of the rooftop longitudinal bench to visiting railway enthusiasts and the children of Fintona.

Over the years, a succession of dedicated one horsepower quadrupeds provided energy efficient 'green' transport and a relaxing ride through the fields. The 'tram' settled down to a daily, except Sunday, routine of meeting all trains at the junction. Fintona Town and Fintona Junction undoubtedly boasted the smallest 'loco sheds' on the Great Northern. Each of these stabling facilities provided fuel in the form of hay, oats and water whilst the indulgent townsfolk contributed carrots, sugar cubes and other tasty morsels. The 'shed' at Fintona Junction also afforded refuge to the branch 'locomotive' from any occasional trauma that might be induced by the sight and sound of the iron horses on the adjacent Omagh–Enniskillen line. As far as can be determined, branch 'locomotives', regardless of gender, were invariably christened 'Dick', although horse brasses incorporating nameplates were never cast at Dundalk works.

Not surprisingly, the Fintona tram came to occupy a significant niche in Irish railway folklore during its later years. Stories about the line abound and two examples will suffice. On one occasion the appearance of a large group of tinkers who crowded into the downstairs saloon on a stormy night caused great consternation among the regular travellers who did not relish the prospect of braving the elements upstairs. The situation was resolved when it was explained to the interlopers that the tram's slow speed uphill to the junction often caused it to miss the Omagh connection – a risk that could be averted by a bracing three quarter mile walk instead. On another occasion in the fifties animal rights activists complained to the GNRI that Dick had the same rights to a holiday as all other company staff.

A concerned management duly dispatched Dick to Bundoran for a week of sea air followed by a week of relaxation in a field adjoining the line. The story has it that Dick broke out of the field and insisted on accompanying the usurper who was performing his work. Old habits died hard on the Great Northern!

As befitted all self-respecting GNRI branch line termini, Fintona station possessed a train shed providing all weather protection. Its short platform with loco shed (stable) incorporated into the premises was unique. Centrally located on the town's main street, the station also offered very limited facilities for freight traffic. The gentle trip to the junction was through a pastoral if unremarkable landscape. Between the rails, both sleepers and ballast were hidden beneath a well worn cinder path etched by horseshoe impressions and a scattering of spent fuel. Fintona Junction was a passing place on the main line with a bay platform for the tram, a waiting room, gents, signal cabin and the branch 'loco shed'. I treasure my memories of arriving there on the footplate of a vintage GNRI 4-4-0 with anticipation growing at the prospect of the forthcoming time warp represented by the transfer from steam to horse traction.

The working timetable allowed 10 minutes for the downhill run to Fintona and 15 minutes for the return journey on the gentle uphill gradient to the junction. The return trip created a unique opportunity for railway photographers to jump off the moving tram, run ahead of it, take their photographs and then rejoin it without threat to life and limb – something I did on a number of occasions.

Assignment to the Fintona branch was not exactly a sinecure for its driver. While Dick seldom needed encouragement – for the single word 'hup' was all that was necessary to start, and the habit of years ensured that Dick made a controlled stop at precisely the same spot at each end of the line – there were some rapid 'loco' reversals necessary at the junction as is evident from the 1957 timetable. Longer intervals there, provided opportunities for Dick to indulge in some unfettered grazing on lush lineside greenery before the return trip to Fintona.

End of the Line

As the sands of time began to run out for the Fintona branch and its GNRI connections, the local populace and the railway enthusiast fraternity became increasingly aware of the treasure they were on the cusp of losing. Visitors from afar, intent on witnessing this wonder, were injecting new life into the little town. The end came at the end of September 1957 when the tram and all connecting services on the Omagh–Enniskillen–Clones line were withdrawn – a very sad day for Co Fermanagh and the adjoining border counties.

If there was one positive element in this last chapter in the history of rail service to Fintona, it was that the Great Northern Railway Board accepted an offer from the Ulster Society for the Prevention of Cruelty to Animals to purchase Dick. He subsequently spent a well earned retirement on a farm at nearby Seskinore, and later in Co Down. One can only speculate as to his success in adapting to a much less structured lifestyle.

Today the citizens of Fintona are served by a Translink bus service to Omagh. Perhaps the Fintona post office still offers those once popular photogravure tram postcards that rail enthusiasts from all over the world used to buy! What was to some eyes an unfashionable relic of yesterday would surely be a tourist attraction today. It is interesting to speculate what the impact on local tourism might have been if it was still possible to take a gentle ride from the town to the junction!

Déjà Vu Down Under

More than fifty years have elapsed since the Fintona tram became history, but apart from a nostalgic reunion with the tram at the excellent Ulster Folk and Transport Museum at Cultra, Co Down and some depressing visits to ruins of the GNRI in the border area, I experienced an astounding sense of déjà vu on the other side of the world in 1981. During a career focusing on branch line and other railway issues in the United States, Canada and Australia, I was heartened to discover a near clone of the Fintona tram in regular service on the tramway linking Victor Harbour, where its still connects with regular preserved steam services, and Granite Island in South Australia. Furthermore, I am happy to report that this antipodal tramway was still literally alive and kicking in February 2004 with no fewer than eleven horses on the roster. All have names but 'Dick' is not amongst them – appropriate perhaps!

Select Reference

Johnston, Norman *The Fintona Horse Tram*: West Tyrone Historical Society, 1993

Acknowledgements

Special thanks are due for additional photographs provided by Trevor Hodge and Gerald Siviour, and the technical assistance of Michael Bowie of Lux Photographic Services, Carleton Place, Ontario. I am also grateful to Jim Kilroy of Howth for reading the manuscript and giving me the benefit of his knowledge of trams.

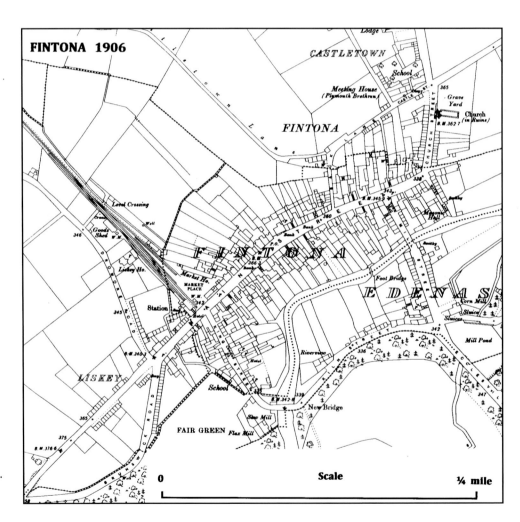

Extract from the 1906 OS map of Fintona showing the town and station. The track layout can be seen in the photo on Page 17.

Omagh-bound shoppers transfer from horse to steam traction at Fintona Junction while Dick appears to have his mind set upon a tasty lineside snack before the return trip to Fintona with Porter Noel Hamilton. Nothing in this busy scene on 7 September 1957 suggests the impermanence of it all, but only three weeks remained before abandonment of not only the Fintona tram but most of the 'Irish North'.

As a mainly interchange point, Fintona Junction offered quite minimal facilities to travellers in contrast to most other stations on the Omagh–Enniskillen line, just a waiting room on each platform and a Gents urinal on the island one. The stable for Dick is visible next to the signal box. The regular tram driver, Willie McClean, always put Dick in the stable during waits at the Junction. Other porters, who did the evening shift, varied in practice as seen in the previous shot.

Disproving the notion that it was always necessary to shut Dick in his stable at Fintona Junction due to his fear of steam locomotives, is this view of Dick waiting to set off for Fintona while passenger interchange from an Enniskillen-bound train is in progress. The unusual carriage on the train is a K9 Brake Third, a former railmotor trailer and one of four of the type. The tram was showing signs of age in 1956.

Trevor Hodge

The uphill journey to Fintona Junction doubtless enhanced the appetite and here Dick is seizing the opportunity for a lineside snack immediately on arrival. Noel has unhitched Dick's harness from the draw chain so that he can graze the lineside. Note the 'swing tree' hanging below his tail. The tram carried quite a bit of light goods merchandise, some of which is stacked on the platform.

GR Siviour

The Great Northern's one horsepower quadruped is working hard on the approach to Fintona Junction with a load of Omagh bound shoppers. This picture illustrates quite well the way the harness worked – a chain on each side linked the collar to the 'swing tree' which in turn was attached to a centrally mounted chain on the tram

As Dick reaches halfway point en route to Fintona Junction it is evident that the driver seldom had to take a hands on approach to his work. With the tram on rails, Dick could hardly veer off to right or left! The seat taken by the small boy epitomizes the delightful informality of this rural byway. On the right is Liskey Cottage, with the town of Fintona in the left background.

Since Dick's ear is just visible, this view was taken on the return journey. Rounding the curve away from Fintona Junction it is clear that a horse tramway was the least intrusive form of public transport in this rural corner of Co Tyrone. To the left of the telegraph pole, we have another glimpse of Liskey Cottage and newer houses along the Dromore Road. Note the soft grit placed over the sleepers – to make things easier for Dick. The tram horses were always called 'Dick' and were usually geldings (neutered males). It is often stated incorrectly that the last, and most famous Dick, was a mare! Stallions were too temperamental to use, but at least one previous tram horse probably was a mare.

GR Siviour

Epitomizing a more leisurely era is this scene of the tram barely disturbing the pastoral tranquillity as it nears the end of another journey to the quiet community of Fintona. In charge on this occasion is the regular 'driver', Willie McClean, though the GNRI gave him only the rank of 'Leading Porter' thus avoiding an engine driver's wage for the man in charge of the horse tram!

GR Siviour

Visiting groups of railway enthusiasts often descended on the Fintona tram during its last years of operation. Here, members of the Cambridge University Railway Circle enjoy the fresh air on a sunny afternoon in June 1956. In the far distance the main street in Fintona runs at right angles to the line and the goods shed can be seen on the right.

Trevor Hodge

A well trodden path occupies the five foot three as Dick gets into his stride on the final part of the downhill run to Fintona. Speeds of six mph had been clocked on this section. Perhaps it was the prospect of refueling at the terminus. With the town in the distance, Liskey Cottage is on the right. The footpath on the right was used by passengers in a hurry!

The presence of seven wagons in the sidings at Fintona suggests the recent visit of a steam hauled goods train. Hoof prints at both sets of points show how Dick tried to avoid crossing the curving steel rail until the last possible moment. The cottage on the extreme right was occupied by Willie McClean and Dick's stable was one of the two sheds with curved roofs that the Singer 1500 car is facing. This view is on 7 September 1957.

Noel Hamilton has the reins firmly in hand as he negotiates the crossover on the approach to Fintona. The tram is passing Liskey House, referred to in the dedication, which is behind the hedge on the left. In later years, Noel became a bus driver and in the 1990s must have been the last bus driver in the British Isles who could claim to have started his driving career on a horse tram! The small open wagon visible in the siding served to carry merchandise and separate the tram (with its overhanging staircase) from a standard goods van when one was being hauled.

Dick makes a dignified departure from Fintona in June 1956 with Willie McClean at the reins This picture gives a good view of the station with its overall roof, which housed the tram at night, and the main street beyond. The pub across the road served as an unofficial 'waiting room'. On the left is the Station Master's house, then occupied by Tom Bradley, the last man to hold the rank in Fintona.

Trevor Hodge

Notwithstanding its short platform, Fintona station offered limited protection from the elements and 'comfort' for male passengers only. On the left, is the goods platform and station yard. Note how, by September 1957, the siding on the right, seen in the previous picture, had been lifted. It was known locally as 'Dora's siding', after Dora Johnston, owner of near-by Liskey House. Today this whole site is occupied by a supermarket.

The stable door is open and Dick is 'coupled up' and ready to leave. The spartan facilities at Fintona were partially ameliorated by the station seat which had apparently migrated from the Junction. Lacking signals, the line was operated for passengers and mixed services on the one horse in harness' basis and 'one engine in steam' for freight. The station notice board carries an unusual poster titled 'Grass on Slopes'.

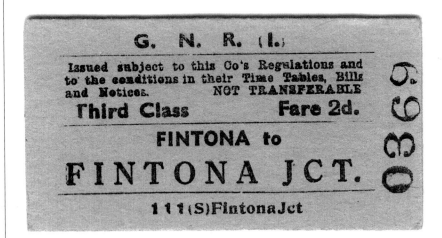

G. N. R. (I.)

Issued subject to this Co's Regulations and to the conditions in their Time Tables, Bills and Notices.   NOT TRANSFERABLE

Third Class   Fare 2d.

FINTONA to

FINTONA JCT.

1 1 1 (S) Fintona Jct

0369

G.N.R. (I.)   DOG TICKET

ONE DOG   Liability not exceeding £2.

FINTONA to

On G N R (I   via

This Ticket must be given up on arrival

Over)   Fare

1076

Visitors would be prepared to pay a lot more than twopence for a ride to the Junction today. The second ticket is for an Omagh-bound dog hauled by a horse that is driven by a man: a perfect conjunction of man and his two best friends.

To the east of Fintona Junction lay the lonely station of Dromore Road, also under the command of Tom Bradley, as was the Junction. On 7 September 1957, P class 4-4-0 No 73 makes a brief stop as it nears the end of its journey from Enniskillen to Omagh. This locomotive dated from 1895.

In this August 1957 view, Dick is safely tucked away in his stable while the ladies of Fintona, intent on an afternoon's serious shopping in Omagh, watch the arrival of PP class 4-4-0 No 12 at Fintona Junction, with a train from Enniskillen conveying more coaches than usual, plus the inevitable bread containers and luggage vans. Note the Fintona branch which is visible on the extreme left.

GR Siviour

On 7 September 1957 the 3.50pm train from Enniskillen has just arrived at Omagh with PP 4-4-0 No 12 in charge. Passengers arriving from Fintona on this service could either continue to Strabane on the adjacent local service, cross the footbridge to await the Belfast bound train or, most likely of all, visit Omagh town to shop. Engine No 12 was built in 1911.

Passengers from Fintona to Belfast switched platforms at Omagh. Here, looking from the Enniskillen end of the station, Q class 4-4-0 No 130, which was built in 1901, has taken water and is about to depart with the 3.50pm Derry–Belfast restaurant car service. This train stopped at Dungannon and Portadown only, with a running time of two hours from Omagh to Belfast Great Victoria Street. No 131 of this class has survived and its restoration is being considered by the Railway Preservation Society of Ireland.

The Granite Island Horse Tram

Déjà vu down under. The Victor Harbour to Granite Island tram at the Granite Island terminus, South Australia on 22 February 2004.

The Granite Island horse tram leaves Victor Harbour and heads for the causeway to Granite Island on 25 August 1991. Something seldom encountered on the Fintona branch was a level crossing used by camels (who give rides for tourists along the beach).

Hill Climbing with the Great Northern

At one time it was possible to escape by tram from the City of Dublin to the peace of the Wicklow mountains, the Liffey valley and to the Howth peninsula. With the passage of time though, the Dublin and Blessington Steam Tramway, the Dublin and Lucan Tramway and the network once operated by the Dublin United Tramways became faint memories. After 1949, the sole survivor was the Hill of Howth tramway which connected the GNRI stations of Sutton & Baldoyle and Howth, via a scenic five and a quarter mile loop line that climbed to the summit of the Hill of Howth (365 feet above sea level) before descending again to the seashore. A further claim to fame was that it was worked exclusively by vintage open-topped trams.

Access to this delightful backwater was by the somewhat irregular GNRI suburban train service from Dublin Amiens Street (now Connolly) to the stations at either end of the tramway. One encountered an interesting array of motive power on this service, ranging from steam and first generation articulated railcars to relatively new AEC diesel multiple units. Many of these services were fill-in turns for trains that normally worked on the main line to Drogheda.

The Howth trains took the Belfast main line for just under five miles before reaching Howth Junction. Travelling from Dublin to Howth in the fifties, the suburbs of Dublin gave way to fields at Killester. After diverging from the main line at Howth Junction, there followed a rural interlude as the train crossed a narrow isthmus connecting the Howth Peninsula to the mainland. The train then arrived at Sutton and Baldoyle Station which served two distinct residential areas. The Howth branch continued eastward for almost a further two miles, hugging the coastline until it terminated beside the harbour at Howth Station, The town of Howth extended up-hill with views overlooking the harbour and the Irish Sea.

This journey from Dublin is still possible but the character of the landscape has been radically changed with suburban development now extending continuously from Dublin to Sutton. The electrified Dublin Area Rapid Transit (DART) trains now provide a frequent service, not only to Howth, but also north to Malahide on the main line to the north. The upland which forms the Howth Peninsula is still a highly desirable oasis of greenery with its golf course, heathland and quality homes, with extensive views southwards over Dublin Bay and northwards to Ireland's Eye and the coast beyond.

In 1959, the fate of the tramway was sealed by the parlous financial condition and demise of its owner the Great Northern. It had failed to make a profit throughout the fifty-eight years of its existence. The tramway took a circuitous but scenic route from Sutton to Howth, which was a leisurely journey of approximately forty-six minutes. It was not an unexpected development when the Great Northern's successor, Coras Iompair Éireann, announced closure, which took place on 31 May that year. There was at that time a widely held view that such a seemingly outmoded form of transport as a tram, should be replaced by what was considered to be the modern and more desirable alternative of a bus service for the many and the private car for the few. Fifty years later the pendulum has swung once again in favour of public transport with a new emphasis on rail services and rapid transit systems. The growth and prosperity, which stemmed from Ireland's membership of the European Union, has dictated major revisions in public transport policy and a rebirth of trams, albeit in a modern form, as an important element in Irish urban transport.

Sutton was the hub of operations and the location of the power plant which supplied the traction current at 550 volts dc until 1934, when the provision of power was taken over by the Electricity Supply Board. Next to the power plant, which stands to this day, and adjacent to the GNRI station, was the car shed which housed the fleet of ten cars working the line and a works car, No 11. An immediate first and favourable impression one received was that of the smart appearance of the trams which, with two exceptions, sported the attractive Oxford blue and cream livery adopted in the thirties in place of their original crimson lake and ivory colour scheme.

Cars Nos 1–8 were 67 seaters which dated from the opening of the line in 1901 and were built by Brush at their Falcon Car Works in Loughborough, England. These trams were fitted with Brill 22E bogies. Cars Nos 9 and 10 appeared in the Autumn of 1902, designed by the GNRI, but built by GF Milnes of Shropshire. These were equipped with Peckham 14D-5 maximum traction bogies but, notwithstanding their slightly larger seating provision for 73 passengers, were less frequently used due to their less stable riding characteristics until after some limited rebuilding in 1958. Whilst Nos 1-8 latterly wore the GNRI Oxford blue and cream livery, Nos 9 & 10 retained the previous varnished grained mahogany finish. Both are preserved – No 9 in the National Transport Museum at Howth and No 10 at the Crich Tramway Museum in England.

 The route of the tramway resembled the path taken by the grand old Duke of York in the well known nursery rhyme (who marched his troops to the top of the hill and marched them down again). The journey began with a brief suburban interlude along Station Road to Sutton Cross, where the Hill of Howth line crossed the former Dublin–Howth route of the Dublin United Tramways. Beyond here, the single track followed the righthand side of the road through a pleasant semi-rural environment as it climbed, punctuated by quite frequent stops, along the Carrickbrack Road. Passing alongside the leafy grounds of Santa Sabina Convent, the tram arrived at the Stella Maris (or Baily View) loop. Here the character of the line changed, with the route cutting across heathland, revealing extensive views over Dublin Bay to the southwest.

A further passing place was encountered at the Summit where trams would normally meet. This was the occasion for a pause and socializing amongst the staff as well as the transfer of any parcels traffic at an adjacent building. Then it was time for the cars to depart for their respective termini at Sutton and Howth. The Hill of Howth was a delightful location with fine views. I admit to feeling some envy at the time for those fortunate enough to live there, especially with a tram service on their doorstep.

For the downhill run to Howth Station the trolley pole was always lowered in the daylight hours and tied down to reduce operating costs, enabling gravity to take hold. Reliance was placed on powerful rheostatic brakes in emergencies. It is unlikely that the contemporary preoccupation with safety and related public liability issues would permit such a practice today, but this was a more relaxed age and there is no record of any disasters. On the run down to Dungriffan Road, wonderful vistas of the islands of Ireland's Eye and Lambay, as well as the coastline beyond, opened up for the delight of those passengers enjoying the fresh air afforded by the open upper deck. Closer to Howth, several sharp curves were negotiated before the tram crossed a road-bridge and deposited its passengers at Howth station, where connections could be made for Dublin. One could of course opt for a bracing walk around the harbour. There was undoubtedly something supremely restful about the Hill of Howth Tramway.

Like the Fintona horse tram, the Hill of Howth Tramway was operated by the Great Northern as an integral part of its five foot three gauge rail network. Sadly, little thought was given by the management to marketing it as a tourist attraction. From today's perspective, its closure appears to have been unfortunate. However, it is necessary to remember that attitudes to public transport have changed. DART has been an undoubted success, Luas (the new Dublin light rail system) has placed Dublin in the forefront of modern urban transit development, and the booming Irish economy has been reflected in rapid urban growth, along with such undesirable side-effects as acute traffic congestion. It is easy to conclude that, had it survived, the Hill of Howth tramway might ultimately have become a valued attraction for Dubliners and visiting tourists alike. Instead, there is some solace to be derived from inspecting the Hill of Howth trams preserved at the National Transport Museum heritage depot at nearby Howth Castle, the Ulster Folk & Transport Museum at Cultra, the National Tramway Museum at Crich, Derbyshire and the Orange Empire Trolley Museum at Perris, California.

Selected references

Flewitt, RC, *The Hill of Howth Tramway*, Transport Research Associates, 1968

Kilroy, James, *Trams to the Hill of Howth*, Colourpoint Books, 1998

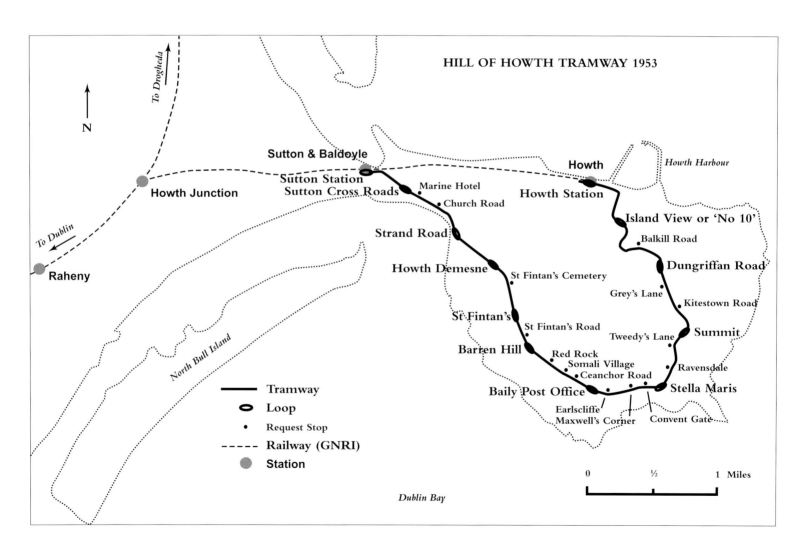

HILL OF HOWTH TRAMWAY 1953

The suburban train service from Dublin to Howth in the pre-DART era was provided on a less frequent basis by the GNRI. T2 class 4-4-2T No 3, built by Beyer Peacock in 1921, arrives at Sutton from Howth with an unusually uniform five-coach suburban rake in August 1958. Although CIÉ was not due to take over until 1 October, the bufferbeam has already been stencilled with its new ownership. Hidden in the stour beyond the wagon is a level crossing at the Howth end of the station.

GR Siviour

In this view, Railcar G, a two-coach unit articulated to a four-wheel central bogie, powered by two 102hp Gardner diesel engines, is leaving Sutton for Dublin Amiens Street (now Connolly) on a service from Howth, on 5 September 1957. To the extreme right is the power house and car shed of the Hill of Howth Tramway. Beyond the distant level crossing gates lies Sutton station – one of two interchange points between rail and tram. The power house ceased to generate electricity for the tramways in the 1930s, after which traction current was supplied by the Electricity Supply Board (ESB).

The Great Northern rostered a variety of diesel and steam power for the Howth services, which added an element of the unpredictability to visits to the Hill of Howth tramway. Here, on 5 September 1957, UG class 0-6-0 No 148, dating from 1948, is assigned a Howth turn at Platform 1, Dublin Amiens Street (now Connolly) This was a bay attached to Platform 2 beyond. GNRI Platforms 3 and 4 are on the left. On the right are the CIÉ platforms, nowadays used by DART services.

Also on 5 September 1957, AEC railcars Nos 618 and 619, plus two K15 open trailers, pause at Sutton and Baldoyle with a Dublin–Howth shuttle service. Although not densely seated for suburban work, these railcars were useful on off-peak services to Howth. The scene, more reminiscent of a quiet country station, is an interesting contrast to the busy DART system of today.

The modest Hill of Howth tram depot at Sutton was adjacent to the station. Car No 4, one of a batch of eight cars delivered in 1901, is just visible within the shed. It is now preserved at the Ulster Folk & Transport Museum at Cultra, Co Down, near Belfast. The railway siding on the right was used to store old coaching stock. Present in this view is an ex-LNWR Brake Third, one of two of the type purchased from the LMS in 1947 and classified L15 by the GNRI.

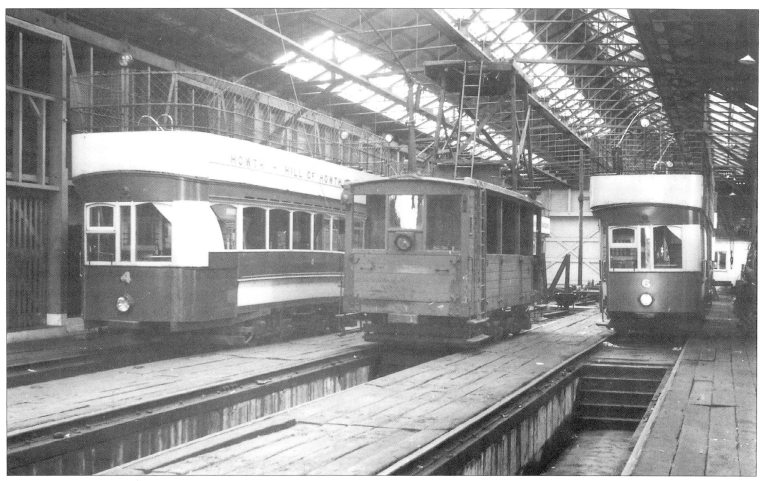

Cars Nos 4, 11, and 6 are occupying the three roads inside the Sutton depot. In common with others of the first batch of eight cars, Nos 4 and 6 were products of the Brush Electrical company and were equipped with two truck-mounted 37½hp Westinghouse motors. Car No 11 sported a faded brown livery and performed maintenance duties throughout its 59 year career. After closure in 1959, car No 4 was transferred to the Belfast Transport Museum, car No 6 was cannibalized for parts by the Tramway Museum Society (for the restoration of Manchester 'Californian' type car No 765), whilst car No 11 remained in storage at the St James Gate Brewery in Dublin before being broken up in 1965. Car No 9 was also stored at the Brewery but was removed to Premier Dairies, Monkstown, Co Dublin, in 1965, by the National Transport Museum and is now on display at their Howth depot, where it is being remotorised.

The interior of car No 7 at Sutton depot, showing the longitudinal seating. Unfortunately this car was not among the survivors following the closure of the tramway in 1959. Car No 7 was the one normally used for driver training and had therefore experienced more that its fair share of 'flats'. It made a clickety, clunk sound in motion and was popularly known as 'the tram with square wheels'.

The field adjoining the Sutton depot was a final resting place for retired Dublin trams waiting hopefully, but in vain, for restoration and preservation. In this case, on 29 March 1953, bogie balcony car No 328 (built by the DUTC at their Spa Road workshops in 1908) and standard four wheel car No 129 (built in 1923 and withdrawn after the closure of the Dalkey route on 9 July 1949) were obviously suffering from the depredations of the local children. Both were eventually scrapped.

Four and a half years later, on 5 September 1957, the field at Sutton was still host to another forlorn relic. On this occasion it was high domed luxury saloon car No 132 (a 1919 product of the Spa Road workshops which had last seen service on the Dalkey route in 1949). It had been brought into the Hill of Howth tram depot in 1952 and fully restored mechanically by motorman Christy Hanaway, and painted by the GNRI staff. In 1953 it was brought into Dublin City and sat proudly beside its old terminus at Nelson's Pillar in O'Connell Street, as part of a Celtic celebration called *An Tóstal*, meaning 'a pageant'. Subsequent to the above photo, the trucks were pushed into a near-by quarry and houses have been built over them. The cottages in the background were the homes of GNRI staff.

We begin our tour of the Hill of Howth system with this view of car No 1 at Sutton station yard on 5 September 1957. Sutton station was accessed by a loop which first crossed Station Road from the tram depot and then recrossed the road onto the tramway's reserved track to reach Sutton Cross. From there trams proceeded to the Summit of the Hill of Howth before descending to the Howth station. Here, No 1 has loaded its passengers and is about to leave the station yard for Sutton Cross.

On a different occasion, in the summer of 1958, car No 6 is seen emerging from Sutton station yard to cross Station Road onto the reserved track. The building on the right is the Station Master's house and the chimneys of the station building can be seen in the background. At that time the Station Master was Fred Millward.

GR Siviour

This is a departing shot of the same tram, showing it setting off along the reserved track towards Sutton Cross in the distance. Note the conductor on the top deck, collecting fares. The tram entered the reserve via the track curving from the left and the points have already been reset. The line disappearing to the right went directly to the tram depot without entering the station. Note the GNRI sidings on the right. This was where horses for the famous Baldoyle Races were decanted and ridden the short distance to the racecourse. The tracks trailed in from the up side, behind the tram depot.

GR Siviour

On 29 March 1953, Summit, or possibly Howth-bound, car No 1 waits at Sutton Cross for boarding passengers. Station Road is on the other side of the low stone wall. As can be seen, there was a passing loop at this point. Sutton Cross was also an interchange point with route 31 of the Dublin United Tramways Company until the closure of their line on 29 March 1941. To avoid the problems of two conflicting sets of 'overhead' the DUTC tramway's wires had a short gap either side of the GNRI line which trams had to coast over. At night time this procedure created a shower of sparks.

Looking in the opposite direction from the top deck of a tram, we see car No 2 entering the loop at Sutton Cross en route to Sutton Station in the winter of 1958. This car has just crossed from Strand Road (now known as Greenfield Road) and is about to pass the tram carrying the photographer. The former Clontarf and Hill of Howth Tramway (latterly DUT), mentioned opposite, ran from left to right across this junction. Priority was determined by the direction of travel of DUT cars. Dublin-bound DUT cars had priority over GNRI cars, but Howth-bound DUT cars had to yield to Summit-bound GNRI cars.

GR Siviour

In this view we are aboard a Sutton Station-bound tram at the Strand Road side of Sutton Cross, looking towards the Sutton Cross loop as car No 6 awaits its arrival. In the left foreground the rails of the former Clontarf and Hill of Howth Tramway are still in situ. Where the two systems crossed the road was cobbled.

GR Siviour

After following Strand Road for some distance, the tramway continued on along Carrickbrack Road. This view was taken from the front of a Sutton-bound tram on the Carrickbrack Road near St Fintans halt in the winter of 1958. The houses now situated on top of the hill to the right are known as 'Somali Village', a name inspired by a model of such a village at the 1904 Dublin Exhibition, where the houses were elevated on stilts to keep snakes at bay. The land on the left is 'Bellinghams' (pronounced 'Belinjums') leading to the middle mountain and the Red Rock bathing place.

GR Siviour

As rumours of pending abandonment spread, the public rediscovered the joys of the Hill of Howth Tramway. Here a well loaded car No 7 climbs towards the Summit along Carrickbrack Road near the St Fintans halt in September 1957. The workman on the right seems to be cleaning the entrance to a private house. There were three 'St Fintans' along the tram route – the Cemetery, the halt or loop, and St Fintan's Road, known locally as the Dell Road.

At Baily View loop, near Stella Maris Convent, the tramway diverged from the Carrickbrack Road to climb inland towards The Summit. In the winter of 1958, car No 7 enters Baily View loop at the start of the climb. The wooden box mounted on the right side of the overhead pole is a Section Box and we can see a lit section light which indicates to the next Sutton-bound tram that the section ahead has been cleared by No 7. Before moving off, the Sutton tram will switch the light to clear the section for him to enter. This will register in a similar section box at the next loop.

GR Siviour

In good weather the upper deck of a Hill tram provided a superb vantage point from which to admire the spectacular views en route to the Summit and to appreciate many of the tramway's finer operating features. The Stella Maris (Baily View) loop was set amidst a profusion of gorse and other heathland vegetation. This picture was taken from car No 1 on 29 March 1953, looking in the opposite direction to the picture on page 49. Carrickbrack Road (Irish for 'speckled rock') is to the right beyond the pole. The house was GNRI-owned and survives as a private residence.

In this view the
photographer
is standing just
beyond the house
at Stella Maris
loop, as Car No 6
descends from the
Summit in August
1958.

GR Siviour

As car No 3 ascends the Hill of Howth near the Summit, it seems likely that the photographer was immortalized on an enthusiast's cine film. In the background is Dublin Bay and the distant Wicklow Hills. The rather austere dwelling behind the tram was called 'Ravensdale' and was then recently constructed. Barely visible above the traction pole to the right is Dalkey Island, with Dun Laoghaire Harbour across the bay. Car No 3 was crewed by Bob O'Connor and Billy Rankin and was known as 'the Christmas Tram' because each year it was festooned with fairy lights, bunting, holly and a Christmas tree.

Against the scenic backdrop of Dublin Bay, a lightly loaded car No 2 tackles the last part of the climb to the Hill of Howth Summit. Although the trams carried boards saying 'Howth – Hill of Howth – Sutton', as seen opposite, the station at the top of the climb was always referred to as 'The Summit'. Car No 2 is now preserved at the Empire Trolley Museum at Perris, California. Old sleepers were used as fencing posts and some are still around fifty years after the closure. The black rectangle at the front of the upper deck was a notice which read "Smokers to sit behind the trolley. No spitting in or on the tram".

Reversible slatted-wood garden seating was the standard passenger provision on the upper deck. The views over Dublin Bay and Ireland's Eye soon distracted the traveller's attention from any shortcomings in comfort. Note that on the Howth trams the trolley standard was offset to the one side with a short bench adjacent. It was always on the seaward side and this car is on the final leg of its journey to the Summit.

Car No 7 has just departed from the Summit loop, on its way to Sutton, in September 1957. It is approaching Tweedy's Lane with its regular motorman, Peter Shiels, at the controls. Old Carrickbrack Road is on the right and the Summit buildings can be seen behind the tram.

Cars Nos 1 and 3 meet and pause at Hill of Howth Summit loop on 29 March 1953. On the right is the waiting room and hidden by No 1 was the parcels office. In the last years No 3 was crewed by Bob O'Connor and Billy Rankin and their courtesy and friendliness made this the most popular tram with regulars. The motorman on No 1 is Tommy Wheelan and he is chatting to what appears to be a visiting inspector.

As well as the wooden parcels office and waiting room, the GNRI provided a bench seat for passengers at the Summit. With no crossing scheduled on this occasion, so car No 7 is running 'wrong road', while three ladies and a child take advantage of the bench. The building on the right is Howth Summit Stores and is still in business, though much enlarged. The house partly obscured by the tram was originally the Summit gatekeeper's cottage. In 1904 the gatekeeper's wife, Mary Waldron, was killed here by tram No 5. Years later, the same tram terminated the mortal existence an unfortunate drunkard, who fell asleep across the tracks near Sutton depot but the crew were exonerated. Not unnaturally, No 5 became known thereafter as the 'unlucky tram'.

After climbing up from sea level at Howth station, car No 3 arrives at the Summit loop on 29 March 1953. The island visible out to sea is Ireland's Eye, a well-known local landmark. Because they were prone to derailments, the two large grained-mahogany cars, Nos 9 and 10, were only used in the summer months and were not allowed on to the steep descent between the Summit and Howth until 1958, when they were fitted with cross-springs from withdrawn Nos 5 and 8. Note the heavily pitted traction pole on the right. In latter years these were filled with concrete and steel rods, but in places the outer shell rusted away to expose the concrete.

Car No 4 climbs away from Dungriffan Road loop, en route to the Summit. The Irish name for Howth is 'Binn Edar' or 'Ben na dair', the Hill of the Oaks. The Danes came in the ninth century and called the place 'Hoved', meaning a headland, and over time this became 'Howth'. This section of reserved track is now a pleasant right of way. The tram has just crossed Grey's Lane.

The view towards Howth from the Dungriffan Road loop, showing Portmarnock Strand in the distance, on the coast north of Sutton. Until recent times, Portmarnock Strand was often used for horse riding.

Car No 1 waits at the tram/rail interchange at Howth Station on 29 March 1953. The platform is just to the left of the tram and was directly accessible through a gap in the wall beside the tram waiting shelter on the left. The main station building is visible on the right. Note the heavy concrete blocks to stabilise the traction poles. The traction pole in the foreground is one of a very few sited on the landward side of the track.

GNRI T2 class 4-4-2T No 62 awaits departure for Dublin Amiens Street, at Howth in the summer of 1958, as Hill of Howth car No 6 unloads after arriving from Sutton. The 4-4-2Ts were an obvious choice for Howth trains but, in the rush hour, even large 0-6-0s were sent out with the heaviest trains. The tanks always worked chimney-first towards Dublin. Facilities at Howth were minimalist for a double track terminus. There was just one platform and a single siding on the seaward side with crossovers between the two lines for running round.

GR Siviour

A set of bell punch tickets sold by the conductor on the Hill of Howth Tramway.

The beautifully restored former Hill of Howth car No 10 at the Crich Tramway Museum on 17 October 2002.

By the same author: All priced at **£8.99.**　　　　Also available (other authors):

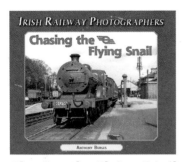

Chasing the Flying Snail
ISBN 978 1 904242 51 2

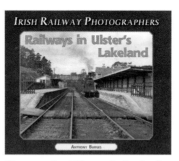

Railways in Ulster's Lakeland
ISBN 978 1 904242 52 9

Steam in Ulster in the 1960s
ISBN 978 1 904242 83 3

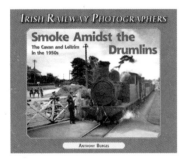

Smoke Amidst the Drumlins
ISBN 978 1 904242 62 8

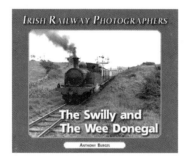

**The Swilly and
The Wee Donegal**
ISBN 978 1 904242 63 5

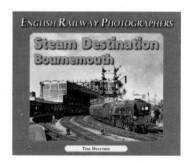

**Steam Destination
Bournemouth**
ISBN 978 1 904242 68 0

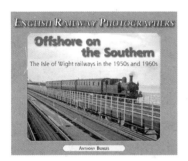

Offshore on the Southern
ISBN 978 1 904242 80 2

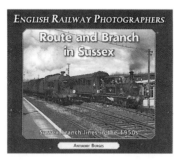

Route and Branch in Sussex
ISBN 978 1 906578 14 5

CIÉ 1958 to 1962
ISBN 978 1 904242 69 7